Dog Overboard

Written by Lisa Thompson
Pictures by Craig Smith and Lew Keilar

Bones, the sea dog, was learning to barrel walk.

It was a new trick and he wasn't very good at it yet.

3

Bones was barrel-walking the top deck when a giant wave hit the ship.

Bones and his barrel bounced off the ship and they were thrown overboard into the sea.

"Dog overboard!" cried Captain Red Beard.

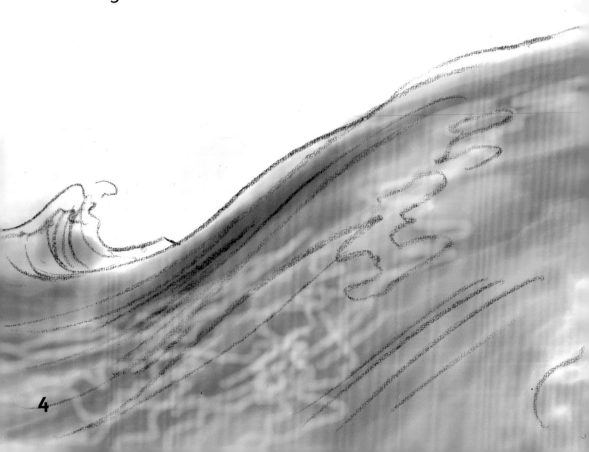

"Help! Help!" yelped Bones.

Lizzie, the first mate, tried to throw Bones
a line, but it wasn't long enough.

The Cook threw Bones a big pot, but it sank.

"Pesky Pirates!" said Fingers, the parrot.

Bones was lost at sea. The waves grew bigger.
Bones was tossed over and over until he felt
seasick.

At last, he climbed on top of the barrel.

Bones surfed the sea.

He drifted on and on away from the ship.

The next morning, Bones and his barrel were washed up onto a small island.

Bones looked all around the island and he found fresh water to drink.

11

Bones had a long sleep on the warm, dry sand, and he dreamed a happy dream about digging for treasure.

When Bones woke up, he had a plan.
He would make a lookout and a bonfire.

Bones searched the jungle and
the beach for wood.

He made a tall lookout and
a large pile of wood.

15

He stood in the lookout and searched the sea for ships.

He saw fish, dolphins, a whale and lots of birds. He did not see a ship.

He waited day and night, night and day. While he waited he practised his barrel-walking trick.

17.

Then early one morning, Bones saw a black dot far out to sea. Bones watched and waited as the black dot grew larger and larger. It was a ship.

Bones lit the bonfire and the ship sailed towards the island.

It was *The Black Beast*!

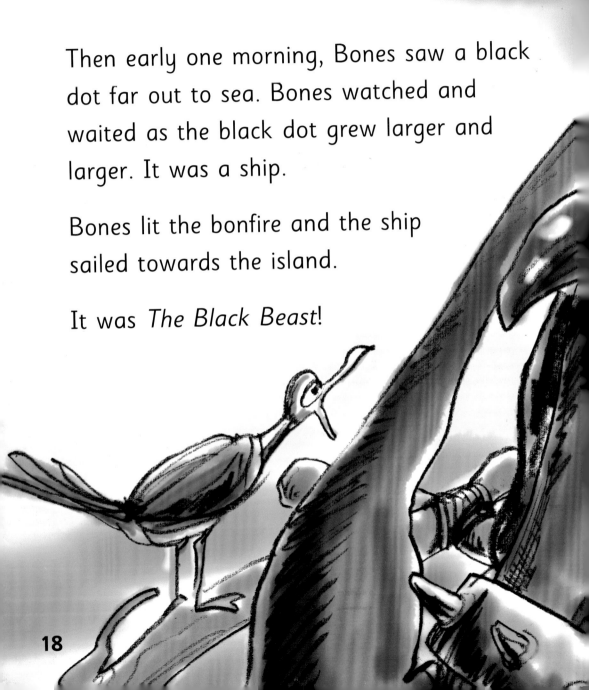

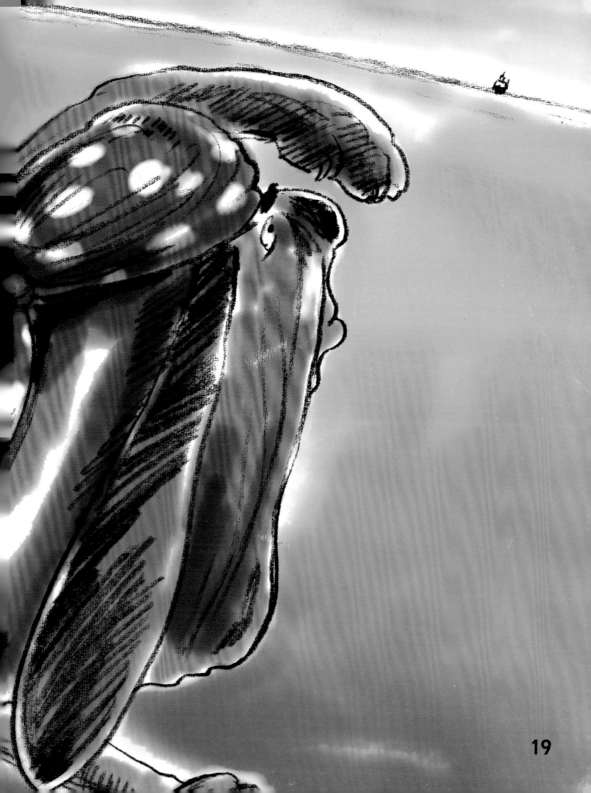

The crew of *The Black Beast* rowed to the beach.

"I've been waiting for you!" barked Bones.

"We searched for you everywhere!" said Lizzie. "Then we saw the fire. What a clever dog you are!"

Bones was rescued.

"Climb aboard!" said Captain Red Beard.
"We've got treasure to find."

"And I've got a new trick to show you,"
said Bones.